"Overcoming The Journey: Battle of The Mind"

Xsánce Love

Copyright © 2021 by Xsánce Littlejohn

Cover Design Copyright © 2021 by T. Fielding-Lowe Media Company

All rights reserved.

"Overcoming The Journey: Battle of The Mind" is based on a true story. Some names and identifying details have been changed to protect the privacy of individuals.

Although the author and publisher have made every effort to ensure that the information in this book was correct at press time, the author and publisher do not assume and hereby disclaim any liability to any party for any loss, damage, or disruption caused by errors or omissions, whether such errors or omissions result from negligence, accident, or any other cause.

No part of this book may be reproduced, stored in a retrieval system, or transmitted in any form or by any means, electronic, mechanical, photocopying, recording, or otherwise, without the prior written permission of the author, except as provided by USA copyright law.

ISBN: 979-8-9887677-3-2

Printed in the United States of America

Xsánce Love is represented by T. Fielding-Lowe Media Company.

T. Fielding-Lowe Company, Publisher

https://www.tfieldinglowecompany.com

I dedicate this book to my Lord and my Savior Jesus Christ, who has been there since day one. Also, to my Mommy for helping me get through my good times and my tough times. To my church family House of Prayer Deliverance Church of All Nations and Bread of Life International Worship Center.

In loving memory of Bishop A.M. Johnson. I would not be a woman of God without you.

In loving memory of Apostle M. Tyrell Neal. You professed things over my life. I know they will come to pass. I know they will.

To anyone and everyone dealing with bullying, depression, anxiety, fear, worry, rejection, and neglect. Remember God is there with you every step of the way.

Table of Contents

Chapter 1………………………………………**Page 1**
How It All Began

Chapter 2………………………………………**Page 8**
When Things Got Worse

Chapter 3………………………………………**Page 19**
When Things Got a Little Better

Chapter 4………………………………………**Page 24**
When My Life Changed

Chapter 5………………………………………**Page 28**
When God Got My Attention

Chapter 6………………………………………**Page 30**
My Heart Change and I Found My Identity

Chapter 7………………………………………**Page 34**
God Can Transform You Too!

Chapter 1
How It All Began

It all began when I was in elementary school. I was in kindergarten at the time. At a young age, I did not have any worries. I had friends and that was most important to me. I was happy. I was good. But I did have this little thought within me that said I was not good enough. I believe that feeling came from the missing relationship with my biological dad. I was missing my dad. I wanted him in my life. My parents were no longer together. I was only two months old when my dad walked away from me. I did not understand why he left.

I had my Mommy though whom I loved. She has always been there for me. However, it was not the same without him there in my life. I always felt like a piece was missing from me. I felt depressed and quietly hid my feelings. No one noticed but my mom because I was a happy and talkative child on the outside. My mom tried her best to help me however, on the inside, I felt depressed.

One day, "I had enough, and I wanted to die. While in class, I said out loud not really talking to anyone specific, "I want to shoot myself". But another student thought I was talking about shooting him. But I was not, I was just voicing my frustrations out loud. I do not know why he thought I was talking about him. Well, either way, I got in trouble. I got called down to the office and sent to speak with a school counselor. I remember a guy who came to get me from class and took me into a room where he asked me questions. I do not remember the name of the guy. All I remember was he was asking me questions and gave me snacks to eat. He gave me Oreos to eat while he talked to me. I do not remember what questions he asked, they were probably about the incident. What stood out for me the most, was me eating the Oreos and him asking me questions.

After that incident at the school, life got a little bit better. I had my best friend that I was able to talk to and share secrets. We were always together and had so much fun together. We were even in the after-school program together. I remember sharing our food and buying each other ice cream or lemonade from the ice cream truck. We both loved the flavor of tiger blood and would get an extra cup so we both could share our favorite lemonade. We split almost everything we had. We were such great friends! All that changed when I moved and was forced to change schools. My best friend gave me peace of mind and an outlet to voice.

I attended school, hung out with friends, and attended after school programs, from first to fourth grade. Until someone found out that I had moved out of the school district and I had to leave that school. I had to leave all my friends, especially my best friend, and go to a new school.

At my new school, Flynn Elementary School, I started to have a hard time. I experienced difficult situations that a child should never go through. I remember it like it was yesterday when all the bullying began to happen.

I was 11 years old in the fifth grade. I had gotten my menstrual cycle for the first time and it happened at school. Instead of someone telling me I have a spot on the back of my pants, they made fun of me, saying that I pooped my pants. That was my first period, and I was still learning how to handle it. I was so embarrassed.

After that, it did not end the bullying kept on going. One day, my grandpa had brought me breakfast from Dunkin Donuts. He had purchased a croissant sandwich made up of bacon, egg, and cheese for me. While I was eating, a piece of the sandwich fell on the ground. Some random kid decided to pick the piece of sandwich off the ground, take a bite, and dropped it back on the ground. He told everyone that I ate it. I knew I did not eat the fallen piece, but I had no evidence that I did not do it. And there were no witnesses either to see them set me up. Because of that situation, I was known as the girl who ate a piece of a sandwich off the ground. Even until this day, I am not sure why someone would eat food off the ground? Especially, since it was wet outside from the rain. I believe that the kid was either hungry or bored. I really do not know why they decided to bully me.

The bullies also made fun of my hair and said that my hair was dirty. One girl brought me some shampoo as to say I did not have shampoo at home, which of course I did. My hair was never dirty and I found it rather rude. Having African American hair, excessive washing can damage

the oils in your hair. After the hair fiasco, another girl decided that she would randomly pick a fight with me. She would hit me then I would hit her back. We fought almost every day after each class we had together. The principal, Mrs. Golderson told me not to hit her back. Like I was not going to defend myself. These fights lasted for weeks to the point that I had marks on my body. My mom and grandpa had to get involved and come to the school. Their presence at the school worked. The fighting finally stopped. But my bully situation did not end there. I believe this same girl was obsessed with me because she would not leave me alone.

Later on in the school year the same girl who I had been constantly in fights with sexually assaulted and began to molested me. She would force me to go into the bathroom with her. She would make me sit on the toilet with my pants down. She would touch me and lick my vagina. Then she made me do it to her. If I did not, she punched me in my stomach, causing me pain. Then she would tell me that she was going to kill me and family to if said anything. When someone would come into the bathroom, she would make me jump on top of the toilet and tell me to be quiet. When I would use the restroom somehow, she would be there too. She would jump on the toilet, look at me, and comment on what I did in the bathroom.

I could not get away from her. It seemed like she was always around me. I was afraid of her and had no escape and could not tell anyone about it. I did not tell my mom until years later because I thought the girl was going kill my mom. I also knew if I told my mom, my mom would have gone to jail. With all this going on, my Dad came back into my life and caused nothing but problems. I could not understand why he came around and would suddenly leave again.

With everything going on, I started to have behavioral problems in school. I was very disorganized, and I ripped up paper in class when I was upset. I felt that was the only way I could express myself. I thought I was not good enough. I thought everyone hated me. You would think things would have changed for me in middle school, but they did not. I was bullied even worse in middle school.

Chapter 2
When Things Got Worse

I remember not wanting to go to school because they made fun of me. They made fun of how I dressed and looked. I did not wear the right name-brands or dressed like a whore as they wanted me. It did not make it any easier when the assistant principal would coordinate lunch lines based on what you wore to school. The better the outfit allowed you to go into the cafeteria first. I would go home crying to my mom, asking her to get me the same clothes. I wanted to be like them. I wanted everything they had.

The bullies would also take my food too. They would ask, "What kind of food do you have today?" They would put their hands in my pockets, take my bags and steal my food from me. If I had brought my lunch; they would take my food off my plate. They would take and eat the food that they liked and leave me with the nasty food. Some days I went home hungry.

I did have some friends, but eventually, they would turn on me. They were pretending to be my friend. They used me for my food and anything else they wanted from me. They were so mean to me. The bullying continued throughout my middle school years. Every day, they would call me names; they told me that I was ugly, that I should kill myself and that nobody loved me. Also, they said I was never going to be anything in this world. They did not let me play or work with them. I was a nice sweet girl who just wanted to fit in. At times I did try to kill myself because of everything that was happening in school. I was beaten up, shoved into lockers and bathroom stalls. When I tried to kill myself the first time, I wrapped my belt around my shoe closet attempting to hang myself. The second time I tried to commit suicide I tried to take pills, but I could not swallow them. A couple of other times, I just kept trying to stab myself in the stomach. Each time, I tried to commit suicide, I felt the hand of God pushing the knife away or keeping me from swallowing. His hand always stopped me from ending my life. I wanted to end my life so bad, but God would not let me. The best thing during those hard time in my life, was my greatest gift, my dog, Arizona. She made me feel a lot better. Arizona was the highlight of my life. She was there through all the hard times in my life. She was there when I tried to kill myself six times. She knew there was something wrong. She would stick by my side. She would always love me. When I was sad, she would lick my tears away. She had her way of helping me through my difficult times. I still had my days though, I wished I would have been dead. I did not understand what was wrong with me.

I asked and asked and searched for help, but no one would help me. Although, my mom did try to help, she went to the schools almost every day. My mom talked to the principals, teachers, and counselors and even tried to sue the school. The teachers, counselors and the assistant principal tried to help by taking me out of the classroom and away from the bullies to give me an escape from them. But that did not work and it just made my situation worse and the bullies angrier and sneakier. One day, I had finally had enough and decided to take matters into my own hands. Up until then, all I did was get in trouble in school for acting out because I was fighting for my life. I got multiple detentions and in-house suspensions. But on this day, I had had enough of it all. I was sitting behind one of my bullies he started to pull my hair and call me names and played with my chair. He told me that I was dumb and stupid. So I got mad and turned around and shoved and smacked him with the book that was on his desk. The teacher saw what I had done to him and sent me to the office. I got suspended from school and he did not get in trouble.

My mom had to go pick me up from school early but I did not get in trouble. My mom was on my side and told me that I should have not done that with a big smile on her face. My mom said she understood why I did it and was happy I finally fought back. But I had no escape. Everywhere I went my bullies were there. You think I would have had an escape when I was not at school, but I did not. To top it off, my grandpa started to call me names. He would force me to eat food that I did not want to eat. I would eat it, and then he would call me fat. But I knew he loved me because he showed me, love. It just made me feel even worse about myself. I knew he would go the extra mile for me. He has always given me anything I needed and has helped to take care of me. Sometimes, he just had a funny way of showing it.

You would think that church would have been a getaway for me, but it was not. I was supposed to be a little angel and God's perfect child in their eyes. My mom was the youth pastor of the church and I was known to be the pastor's child. They would not let me do anything I wanted because I was supposed to be the good one.

The youth at the church put me on this high pedal stool. I was a child, just like them. When they said they wanted to go to the clubs, parties, and stuff like that, I said I wanted to go. They would say you cannot do that.

Anything that did not have something to do with God, they would tell me I could not do. While at church if I got a biblical question or activity wrong; they would ask me why I got the answer wrong and tell me that I should know the whole Bible. But I was learning at the same time they were. What made it even more difficult was my church was a deliverance ministry, and deliverance ministries encounter things other ministries do not. In deliverance ministry, I was taught and learned a lot of things other ministries did not know about. I wanted our church to be like the other churches I had seen and do what they did.

The other thing that upset me about attending my church was my grandmother went to the same church and had has some mental issues. My church family would support my grandmother and take her side, but they did not understand what was happening behind the scenes. They would make me feel bad for what I said or did to her. The church only saw the one side of my grandmother she showed them. They never got to see the other side of her when she was alone with my mom and I. That made me feel even worse. My bishop, Bishop A.M. Johnson, who had known what was really going on with my grandmother, unexpectedly passed away leaving no one except my myself and mother to deal with what was going on at church. My Bishop had supported my mom and I and understood our dilemma. Even though there were some hard times, there were so many fun times at church as well. We had cookouts, birthday parties, dinners, and special services for the youth. Back then church was all day on Sundays and after the long days at church, we would all go out to a restaurant to eat together, which I really enjoyed. I had a love hate relationship with my church but I am grateful for the experiences there because they helped shape me into the woman I am today.

You would think it could not get any worse, but it did. I almost lost my mommy. I remember I was at my house. My nana lived upstairs on the third floor, and my mom and I lived downstairs on the second. My mom had not been feeling well for a few days and had gotten worse. My mom asked me to call my nana to take her to the hospital. I stood in the hallway, yelling for my nana. I told nana to take my mom to the hospital. Instead of taking her to the hospital, she called 911.

When the ambulance came, they took my mom to the hospital. I was so worried that I was going to lose my mommy. She was fighting for her life. When I saw her slowly dying at the hospital, I did not know what I would do. I remember asking God to please save my mom. She stayed in the hospital for a few weeks. She was sick for a while. When my mom was released from the hospital she was home finally. It made me feel better, but I still had the thought that I might lose my mom because she was still sick. I could not understand why everything was happening to me. And on top of it all the school required me to begin sessions with the school counselor every day.

My mother was still battling the illness that had put her in the hospital she was unable to drive and I had to take the city bus to get to school. The bus driver was a woman I believe God sent to watch out for me. My mother and I were nervous about me taking the bus alone. On the days leading up to my solo city bus ride, my mother rode the bus with me a few times in order to show me what to do. The same woman drove the bus each time. The bus driver told us if she saw me on her bus she would look out for me. And she did, she would wait for me if I was running late and even pulled the bus in the middle of the street to stop the traffic so I could cross the street. One of the best things I remember her doing was on a day it was pouring rain outside and she dropped me off right at my front door. Each time I would ride the bus I would wave goodbye to my mother watching in the window and the bus diver would too.

On one of my bus rides to school I met a lovely lady named Mrs. White. Meeting with her made school a bit easier for me. We rode the bus together and it was fun. I would look forward to seeing her every day. Mrs. White would always encourage me and make me feel better. Sadly, she passed away before I went to high school.

Chapter 3
When Things Got a Little Better

Things started to change when I went to high school. However, I was still struggling with the aftermath of the bullying crisis. At times I could still hear the echoes of the sounds of their voices in my head. After all those years dealing with it, they didn't go away instantly. I still heard the bullies' voices in my head saying," You will never be anything in life. You should go kill yourself. Your ugly, nobody loves you, nobody wants you, you're never going to achieve your goals, and you can't do it."

During my first year of high school, I had a hard time trusting people. I met new people, and some tried to bully me. However, this time, I did not allow it! I spoke to the school deans and they took action immediately, unlike my last schools. My years of high school were ok, but I still did not feel good enough. I was not sure of who I was. I was trying to be like everyone else and not be myself. Honestly, I did not want to be me. I thought there was something wrong with who I was. I was trying to be like everyone else. I was not sure who Xsánce was and what my life's purpose.

My church ended up closing down, which made things a bit difficult. I ended up going to a church, where I was not growing. It was not the same experience as my previous church. I did not feel the love of a church family from that church. At that church it felt totally different and distant. I felt like I was a random stranger out on the street. Then God sent my mom and I to another church. This church was better for me. I began to grow again, the atmosphere was loving, and I felt included.

Everything changed during my senior year in high school when I finally realized for myself without being told, who I was and how much God loved me. I was growing and learning spiritually. I wish I would have known then what I know now, that it was all going to be over soon. However, from time to time I would still have those lying thoughts in the back of my mind I was still going through it. But a significant change happened after high school.

First, I went to a new church which was ok, but I did not really like it. I felt I was not growing. It made me feel it was ok to do whatever I wanted in life and then just repent for the sins. I was not doing anything in ministry. The children in the youth group were not friendly either. My mom and I stopped going to that church and God led us to a different church; where I was able to grow. It reminded me of my old church, and gave me that feeling of love and care I had missed. I started to remember who I was again. But I still wanted to act up a bit in college. I had made up my mind I was going to have fun. God was pulling me to Him, but I decided to ignore him. I was determined to act a fool while I was in college, I was going to drink, smoke, and party.

I was going to take a break or leave church, because I had spent my whole life in church. I knew I could not live a double life, partying and being Christ like at the same time. I spoke to people about my dilemma. Some people said I should party and some said I should not. I wanted to experience life for myself. But I still loved God. However, I wanted to live both lifestyles and I tried to. When I graduated from high school, "it was on and poppin'!"

Chapter 4
When My Life Changed

In my first year of college, I had decided to do my own thing. I did not want anything to do with God. During my spring semester, I stayed on campus and that's when I started to try all the things I had been planning. I had roommates who encouraged me to experiment. They tried to get me to smoke, drink, or go to parties and have sex. I was interested in all those things because I wanted to do everything opposite of what I was taught even though knew what was right.

One night, we smoked weed and got high, but it was not that bad of a high and ended up smoking hookah and e cigarettes as well. I ended up having a bad headache after I smoked. On a different occasion my roommates and I smoked for a second time. It was not that bad at all either. But the third time was the worst of them all. I remember we went to the little corner store to buy paper for the weed, after we got the weed we smoked it. We each shared three blunts. I coughed for a while my head began to spin, I was high. I was in the elevator talking to my roommate. My roommate and I sounded like we had sucked the helium out of a balloon. Our voices were so high. She kept asking me if it was good. I said yes. But after that experience, I felt guilty for smoking.

Once I got back to our room, I began to panic. I remember eating and praying. My roommates were starting to get mad at me and wanted me to shut up. I prayed about 20 times that night. I went to bed and tried to go to sleep, but I was still freaking out. My chest was hurting, so I end up going to the hospital for the pain. The doctor said that I was dehydrated and that I had heartburn. I went home after I left the hospital.

I did not tell my mom about the weed I smoked that night I only told her my stomach was bothering me and I couldn't eat certain foods anymore. But you would have thought that I would have learned my lesson. Nope. When I got back on campus, I decided to go to a party at the Student Union. My roommates and I planned out our outfits for the party. We even practiced dancing for it too. All of this was happening the week of Resurrection Sunday (Easter Sunday).

I called my mom, asking if I should go to the party. I had started attending my new church and had the responsibility of being an example to the youth. I could not decide. I was torn between the two. I wanted to go to a college party so I could have that experience. Well, I had gone to a college party before but not one as big as this one at the Student Union.

My mom was not happy at all and did not want me to go to a party, but she left it up to me to decide. I knew I could not let my roommates down, so I decided I was going to go. Until I saw my advisor and he asked what my plans were for the weekend. I responded by saying, "I'm going to go to the union party". Afterward he said, "You're going to go to a party then go to church on Sunday." I said yes. He said," well, I'm not going to tell you what to do. Do what you want." He made me feel even guiltier. So, I did not go to the party. I went to the church service. As much as I tried to act differently and do the wrong things, the Holy Spirit would not let me.

God was still pulling and calling me while I tried and failed to live two lifestyles. I knew I had a calling on my life, but I was still trying to fight it. I finally had to choose whether I was going to live for God or the devil.

Chapter 5
When God Got My Attention

During my second year of college, was when I was able to experience God for myself. I began going more to this group named Sankofa. Sankofa is an anointed Christian group on campus. When I went to that Christian meeting, the love of God was there, and I felt it. This group showed me other people like me are going through the same things I was experiencing. Sankofa was like a family to me. The students that participate in this group shared the same faith as I do. They welcomed and encouraged me when I needed it the most. If I required prayer, they were there to pray with me.

Going to Sankofa, showed me that not all people were rude. I met this girl while attending this group. She was one of the people who helped on the e-board. She would encourage me to do good things and would also talk me out of doing bad things. Which gave me more motivation about my decision to follow Christ.

I would still do some things she advised me not to, because I did not start listening to her advice until later in college. I had to change to another school during my sophomore year of college, but I still attended Sankofa and spent time with her.

When I decided to change my life for God entirely. I still felt I was missing something. It was Valentine's Day, which was a day that I hated. However, that particular Valentine's Day was different. I planned to go out with some friends and try to get with this guy that I liked. That plan did not work out. I ended up staying home that night. I was so upset. I was still hurting inside and I remember crying on the floor in my room when I heard God's voice saying I love you and I got you, my daughter. It's going to be ok. At that moment, I began to cry even more. From that day, I knew God was with me, and that was when I let God take control of my life.

Chapter 6
My Heart Change and I Found My Identity

Ever since, I gave my life to Christ and had my own experiences with God. My life has changed. I finally found myself. I know who I am. I have grown so much spiritually. I know what my purpose in life is. I still hear the negative voices trying to come back to my mind, but they are very faint. They no longer influence me. Overtime, I cannot even understand what they were saying.

I knew who I was now. I loved myself for me. I did not care about what people said. I cared about what God said. After, I gave everything completely to God and no longer held anything back I was able to grow, find myself, and purpose. With the help of my church and the Christian group I was able to start fresh and not have anyone judge me. They liked me for me.

My life changed. I prayed more and started to read more. I focused on who I was in Christ and not what everyone else thought. I realize God's words matter. I knew if he brought me this far that I can do anything. God was always there when I needed him. He provides for me. He always has ways of showing how much he loves me. I had to learn to trust him, and give my all to him and allow him to take control over my life.

When I allowed God into my life, I felt better than ever. I still go through struggles, but God is there every step of the way. I had to learn how to humble myself and know that I cannot do this independently. Without God by my side, I would keep falling on my face. I got tired of going through the same cycles all the time.

You are going to mess up and have trials. You are not perfect. Jesus was the only perfect man on earth. When you get back up on your feet and give it to God. He knows how you feel and wants to hear from you. I learned that. That is why I pray and talk to God about everything. It makes me feel better. God gives me peace. He cares for me, and I know he will never leave me. Once, I entirely gave him control, my life changed. I do not regret it because I feel better than I have ever felt before.

You probably think this God thing is not real and that it was just me. But I am telling you how God has changed my life. I know from experiences if God had not sent people in my life to help me. I would probably still be going through the same struggles in life, or I would not have been here to share my story with you. God is still writing my story, so it is still continuing. And he uses me to share what I have been through so I can help you. This is not the end of me. I have so much more to do in life.

Chapter 7
God Can Transform You Too!

I want you to know that you are ok. God is there with you. All you must do is give your life to him. He does not care about what you have done because he loves you. He wants to take away all the pain, clean you up, and be there for you. I invite you to say this prayer with me.

"Father God, I am a sinner. I believe Jesus is the son of God. I believe Jesus died on the cross and rose from the dead for my sins. I believe Jesus is Lord. Help me to live this life for you. I cannot do this on my own. I want you to come into my life and make me whole. Thank you, Lord, for saving me. In Jesus' name Amen. It is that simple, and now you are saved.

Now the angels are having a party in heaven because you have become part of the family. God loves you. The most significant thing to remember is when we fall, he will pick us up. If you ran away and came back. He will welcome you with open arms and throw a party for you. God is a God of love and cares for you when no one else does. He will take care of you. I did not have my biological dad in my life, however I have God as my father. He provides and takes care of me. God had blessed me even when I did not even deserve it.

He knows how many hairs we have on our heads. He will send someone or something just to make you happy. If he did it for me, he could do it for you. I could not imagine my life without him. God has made my life better. I am proud to say that I am a suicide survivor and happy to say I will never try to kill myself again. I do have my days when I feel weak, but I know that everything will be ok with God on my side.

I know my father is happy with me because he makes sure to show me that he loves me every day. He sends me unconditional love and makes me feel good. I have trials and tribulations, but I know one day this will all be over. I know who I am in Christ. I am a powerful woman walking in destiny and purpose. You should know you are a woman or man of destiny and purpose. We are royalty. We are kings, queens, princes, and princesses of the kingdom of God. We are strong and we never give up. All we need to do is trust in the Lord God. Remember to worship and praise, read the bible, pray every day, and go to church. It is going to be ok hold on, my sister, my brother. God is on his way and it is not over yet. He is still writing our stories. Stay tuned and see what happens next with the me, Xsánce!!!!:)

SINNER'S PRAYER

Father, I know that I am a sinner, and I ask for Your forgiveness. I believe You died for my sins and rose from the dead. I turn from my sins and invite you to come into my heart and life. I want to trust and follow You as my Lord and Savior. In Jesus' name Amen.

Here are few scriptures I would like to share with you to give you some encouragement.

Philippians 4:13

John 15:17

Proverbs 3:5

Psalms 139

Psalms 23

Psalms 27

Romans 12:2

Isaiah 41:10

Joshua 1:9

1 Peter 2:9

Ephesians 1:1-4

Jeremiah 1:5

Jeremiah 29:11-12

2 Corinthians 4:16-18

Deuteronomy 7:6

Colossians 3:12-17

ABOUT THE AUTHOR

My name is Xsánce Love Littlejohn and I love to try to make people smile through their tears. Helping people is an important part of my life as is spreading the word of Jesus. Because I've been through tough times in my life, I understand the importance of being a helping hand to others suffering their own darkest moments. Seeing people laugh brings me immeasurable joy and I hope to be a light in the dark for someone needing it most.

I'm from the best and smallest state, little old Rhode Island. When I'm not busy spreading Jesus' teachings, I enjoy singing and acting. Sharing my life's story is my way of helping other young people to understand they're not alone no matter what they're facing. Having faced my fair share of bullies and rejections. I can understand why youth and young adults today are dejected, scared, and sad. Life is tough, but we're tougher. With God on our side, we can come through anything.

Let's stay connected! Follow me on Facebook at Author Xsánce Love and Instagram at @XistheX.

www.ingramcontent.com/pod-product-compliance
Lightning Source LLC
LaVergne TN
LVHW061049070526
838201LV00074B/5232